GROUNDHOG DAY UNVEILED

Cultural References and Pop Culture:

Groundhog Day in Film and TV

CINDY R. DESROSIERS

TABLE OF CONTENTS

<u>INTRODUCTION</u>

<u>CHAPTER 1: WHEN DID GROUNDHOG DAY ORIGINATE?</u>

<u>- Outline of Groundhog Day</u>

<u>- Verifiable Importance</u>

<u>CHAPTER 2: THE GROUNDHOG'S EXPECTATION</u>

<u>- Examination of Punxsutawney Phil's Estimate</u>

<u>- Influence on Climate Forecasts</u>

<u>CHAPTER 3: FESTIVITIES ALL OVER THE PLANET</u>

<u>- Merriments and Customs</u>

<u>- Groundhog Day Occasions</u>

<u>CHAPTER 4: GROUNDHOG DAY IN MAINSTREAM SOCIETY</u>

<u>- References in Motion pictures and Programs</u>

<u>- Critical Minutes</u>

CHAPTER 5: GROUNDHOG DAY RECIPES

- Winter-themed Dishes

- Groundhog-molded Treats

CHAPTER 6: GROUNDHOG DAY REALITIES AND FANTASIES

- Exposing Normal Convictions

- Uncommon Groundhog Day Stories

CHAPTER 7: NATURAL VIEWPOINTS

- Groundhogs and Environments

- Preservation Endeavors

CHAPTER 8: GROUNDHOG DAY IN 2024

- Features of the Day's Occasions

- Public Responses and Online Entertainment Buzz

CONCLUSION

INTRODUCTION

Welcome to the investigation of Groundhog Day! This particular custom, celebrated yearly on February 2, taught the creative minds of individuals all over the planet. Groundhog Day is something beyond an unusual occasion; it's a novel expectation, climate expectation, and local area festivity.

In this excursion, we'll dig into the starting points and meaning of Groundhog Day, unwind the fables encompassing Punxsutawney Phil, and the notable groundhog, and investigate the merriments that make this day a social peculiarity. From the development service to the web-based entertainment buzz, participate in the festival of this beguiling and now and again erratic custom.

CHAPTER 1: WHEN DID GROUNDHOG DAY ORIGINATE?

- Outline of Groundhog Day

"Groundhog Day" is a 1993 parody show movie coordinated by Harold Ramis. The story rotates around Phil Connors, a negative and conceited meteorologist depicted by Bill Murray. Phil is doled out to cover the yearly Groundhog Day occasion in Punxsutawney, Pennsylvania, where a groundhog named Punxsutawney Phil predicts the climate.

Nonetheless, Phil winds up caught in a period cycle, compelled to remember February Despite than once. Despite his underlying dissatisfaction and endeavors to take advantage of the circumstance, Phil bit by bit goes through a groundbreaking excursion. As he encounters similar occasions again and again, he begins gaining from his missteps and turns into a more merciful and mindful individual.

The film dives into topics of existentialism, personal development, and the results of one's activities. Phil's dull encounters permit him to break liberated from his egocentric outlook and foster certifiable associations with individuals around him. He figures out how to see the value in the worth of benevolence, compassion, and magnanimity.

The supporting cast incorporates Andie MacDowell as Rita, Phil's maker, and Chris Elliott as Larry, a cameraman. The film's smart screenplay, combined with Bill Murray's excellent presentation, has added to "Groundhog Day" turning into a perseverance of art. It is perseverance through request lies in its mix of humor, contemplation, and the ageless message that self-improvement and significant change are reaching the dullest and testing conditions.

- Verifiable Importance

"Groundhog Day" has acquired verifiable importance as a social standard in the domain of film. Past its diversion esteem, the film has turned into an illustration of individual change and the potential for positive change. The persevering through fame and basic praise have raised it to famous status.

Groundhog Day

The film's investigation of existential topics about the way of thinking about personal development has resonated with crowds. "Groundhog Day" fills in as a special editorial on the human experience, underscoring the significance of compassion, graciousness, and self-improvement. Its immortal message has prompted its consideration in conversations on the way of thinking and brain science.

Besides, the expression "Groundhog Day" itself has entered the vocabulary as an illustration of a circumstance that appears to perpetually rehash. This social effect stretches out past the film, impacting conversations on the idea of time, schedule, and the opportunities for change in one's life.

In 2006, the US Public Fchosenservation Board chose "Groundhog Day" for protection in the Public Film Library, perceiving its social, verifiable, and tasteful perseverance The film's perseverance through fame and its capacity to ignite significant discussions add to its authentic significance in the realm of film and mainstream society.

CHAPTER 2: THE GROUNDHOG'S EXPECTATION

- Examination of Punxsutawney Phil's Estimate

Punxsutawney Phil's weather conditions figure on Groundhog Day is a capricious custom established in legends. As per the practice, on the off chance that Phil sees his shadow, there will be six additional lifters; in late winter that is not, a late winter is anticipated.

From a meteorological viewpoint, Phil's gauge is simply emblematic and not in light of logical proof. Weather patterns on a particular day in February are not characteristic of the more extensive occasional examples. The possibility of a groundhog foreseeing the weather conditions is a happy and engaging part of the Groundhog Day festivity.

The custom has persevered for more than 100 years, catching the public's creation-loving and adding a fun-loving component to the social recognition of Groundhog Day. It fills in as a sign of the association between nature, fables, and local area festivities, regardless of whether the exactness of the forecast is simply unplanned.

- Influence on Climate Forecasts

Punxsutawney Phil does note that Groundhog Day does not affect the field of logical climate expectatiogaugingther conditions information-driven and information-driven process that includes investigating different meteorological variables, satellite symbolism, PC models, and verifiable example cutting-edge use cutting edge innovations and logical techniques to give precise and dependable weather conditions figures. These gauges depend on constant information, barometrical circumstances, and computational models that mimic the way of behaving of the climate.

The Groundhog Day custom, where Phil's shadow probably predicts the approaching climate, is a social and folkloric occasion instead of a logically grounded forecast. Phil's activities on a particular day in February make little difference to the air conditions or weather conditions that impact long haul weather conditions conjectures.

In established researchers, climate expectations are constantly refined and worked on through progressions in innovation and a more profound comprehension of barometrical cycles. Punxsutawney Phil's estimate remains a beguiling custom, however, it contributes no significant proof-based thorough and proof-based area of meteorology.

CHAPTER 3: FESTIVITIES ALL OVER THE PLANET

- Merriments and Customs

Groundhog Day merriments and customs revolve around well-known Phil, the well-known groundhog from Punxsutawney, Point-by-pointer is a point-by-point clarification:

1. Groundhog Prediction: The headliner Phil rises out of 2nnel on February secondaries; if Phil sees his shadow, there will be six additional long stretches of winter. On the off-chelate winter doesn't, a late winter is anticipated. This expectation is reported during a function in Punxsutawney.

2. Punxsutawney Celebration: The town of Punxsutawney has a progression of occasions paving the way to large Groundhog Day. A large number of individuals observe Phil's expectations. The festival incorporates music, diversion, food, and a happy climate.

3. Affirmation: after rising out of his tunnel, Phil "conveys' ' his expectation to the Groundhog Club president in "Gro" a language figured out by the inward circle. The president then deciphers Phil's directive for the group.

4. Groundhog Club's Inward Circle: A gathering of neighborhood dignitaries known as the Internal Circle sorts out and manages the occasions. They are liable for dealing with Punxsutawney Phil consistently and assume key parts in the Groundhog Day merriments.

5. Weather Capital of the World: Punxsutawney gladly alludes to itself as the "Climate Capital of the World" because of the consideration collected by Groundhog Day. The occasion draws in media inclusion from around the globe.

6. Groundhog Day Film Influence: The prominence of the film "Groundhog Day" has added to the celebrations. A few occasions might incorporate references to the film, and it has become entwined with the social festival.

7. Local and Worldwide Celebrations: While Punxsutawney is the focal point, different spots across North America and the past observe Groundhog Day with their nearby groundhogs making forecasts. Every area puts its exceptional twist on the practice.

- Groundhog Day Occasions

Groundhog Day occasions are based on the expectations made by Punxsutawney Phil, the renowned groundhog from Pennsylvania. Here is a definite clarification of the key components:

1. Emergence Ceremony: The headliner happens almost immediately on the morning of February 2 in Punxsutawney. A huge group accumulates at Gobbler's Handle, a rustic region where Phil's tunnel is found. Phil is persuaded out of his tunnel, and the group enthusiastically anticipates his climate expectation.

2. Phil's Prediction: As Punxsutawney Phil arises, the group observes near checks whether he sees his shadow. Assuming he does, custom

holds that there will be six additional long stretches of winter. If he doesn't, a late winter is anticipated. Phil "imparts" his expectation in "Groundhogese," and the Internal Circle deciphers it for the crowd.

3. Inner Circle Involvement: The Internal Circle, a gathering of neighborhood dignitaries, assumes a critical part in sorting out and directing the occasions. They are liable for Phil's consideration and direction of the merriments, adding a component of function and custom to the procedures.

4. Preceding Festivities: Paving the way to the headliner, Punxsutawney has a progression of merriments including music, diversion, food sellers, and an overall merry air. Guests originate from all over to take part in the festivals.

5. Global Recognition: The Punxsutawney occasion gets broad media inclusion, transforming the modest community into a point of convergence on Groundhog Day. Media sources and telecasters from around the world cover the expectation function.

6. Cultural References: The occasions frequently incorporate references to the film "Groundhog Day," for certain festivals integrating components from the film into the merriments. This adds a layer of mainstream society to the conventional procedures.

7. Local Groundhogs: While Punxsutawney Phil is the most renowned, different areas have their groundhogs making forecasts. Every nearby groundhog occasion follows a comparative

organization with an emphasis on development
and forecast.

CHAPTER 4: GROUNDHOG DAY IN MAINSTREAM SOCIETY

- References in Motion pictures and Programs

"Groundhog Day" has transformed mainstream society, with references showing up in different motion pictures and Programs. Here are a few eminent models:

1. The Simpsons (Television Show): The episode named "Bart Gets Grounded" highlights a Groundhog Day subject where Bart is trapped in a period cycle, remembering that every day over and over.

2. Supernatural (Television Show): In the episode "Secret Spot," the Winchester siblings

experience a period circle, and one of them continues to remember that very day, suggestive of the Groundhog Day idea.

3. Happy Passing Day (Film): This ghastliness parody film takes a Groundhog Day bend, highlighting an understudy who remembers the day of her homicide over and over, attempting to find the personality of her executioner.

4. Star Trip: The Future (television Show): The episode "Circumstances and logical results' includes the group of the USS Endeavor encountering a period cycle, rehashing similar occasions, like the reason for Groundhog Day.

5. Xena: Fighter Princess (Television Show): In the episode named "That is old news," Xena and Gabrielle figure out themselves in an

opportunity circle, remembering a day with silly and heartbreaking results.

6. Russian Doll (Television Show): This Netflix series follows a lady who continues kicking the bucket and remembering her 36th birthday celebration, investigating subjects like Groundhog Day.

7. Edge of Tomorrow (Film): While not an immediate reference, this science fiction film featuring Tom's Journey includes a person encountering a period cycle, and confronting comparable difficulties over and over.

- Critical Minutes

"Groundhog Day" is loaded with critical minutes that have become notable in realistic history. Here are some champion scenes:

1. Phil's Passionless Routine: The film starts by laying out Phil Connors' daily practice, accentuating his pessimistic and unresponsive demeanor toward his work and the individuals around him. This makes way for his change.

2. Ned Ryerson Encounter: Phil's rehashed experiences with Ned, the excessively excited protection sales rep, become a running gag. The communications catch Phil's disappointment with the tedium of his day.

3. Phil's Careless Behavior: As Phil understands the results are immaterial, he participates in wild and clever exercises, from pigging out to taking a groundhog and driving on train tracks.

4. Learning the Piano: With an end goal to intrigue Rita, Phil figures out how to play the piano. The scene where he faultlessly performs "Composition on a Topic of Paganini" exhibits his developing personality.

5. Helping Others: Phil begins utilizing his time circle to assist with peopling in the town, saving a man from gagging, fixing a punctured tire, and performing different thoughtful gestures. These minutes mark his shift from self-centeredness to unselfishness.

6. Groundhog Day Montage: The montage portraying Phil's rehashed days set to "I Got You Darling" by Sonny and Cher has turned into a notorious arrangement, catching the recurrent idea of his situation.

7. Ice Model for Rita: Phil's genuine endeavors to prevail upon Rita come full circle in a delightfully created ice mold. This motion denotes a defining moment in their relationship.

8. Phil's Transformation: The scene where Phil awakens to find it February third, flagging the finish of the time circle, exhibits his total change into a superior individual.

CHAPTER 5: GROUNDHOG DAY RECIPES

- Winter-themed Dishes

Winter-themed dishes frequently embrace good, warming flavors and ameliorating surfaces to battle the chilly climate. Here is a definite investigation of some colder time of year-propelled culinary joys:

1. Soup Varieties:

   Winter is inseparable from soothing soups. Works of art like generous vegetable soup, chicken noodle soup, and rich tomato bisque give warmth and sustenance during cold days.

2. Stews and Casseroles:

Slow-cooked stews and dishes are staples in the colder time of year kitchen. Whether it's a meat stew, chicken pot pie, or a rich vegetable goulash, these dishes offer a delightful mix of flavors.

3. Roasted Vegetables:

Root vegetables like carrots, parsnips, and yams sparkle during winter. Broiling them with spices and olive oil improves their regular pleasantness, making for a scrumptious and nutritious side dish.

4. Braised Meats:

Braising harder cuts of meat in appetizing fluids, similar to red wine or stock, produces delicate and tasty outcomes. Pot broils braised short ribs, and coq au vin are well-known decisions for winter eating.

5. Savory Pies and Quiches:

Winter calls for flavorful pies loaded up with fixings like meat, mushrooms, or turkey. Quiches with occasional vegetables and cheddar make for a flexible and fulfilling feast.

6. Hot Pot and Fondue:

Warm collective dishes like hot pot and fondue unite individuals throughout the cold weather months. These common encounters include cooking fixings at the table in a tasty stock or liquefied cheddar.

7. Pasta and Risotto:

Rich and velvety pasta dishes, like Alfredo or carbonara, give solace in the colder months. Also, generous risottos with fixings like butternut squash or wild mushrooms are winter's top choices.

8. Baked Goods:

Winter is the ideal time for liberal heated products. Consider cinnamon rolls, gingerbread treats, and warm organic product shoemakers. These treats carry a feeling of comfort to the season.

9. Mulled Beverages:

Thought about wine, juice, or even tea with warm flavors like cinnamon, cloves, and nutmeg are famous winter refreshments. They give a consoling warmth as well as inspire the bubbly soul.

10. Chocolate-based Desserts:

Winter calls for debauched treats, and chocolate plays a featuring job. Whether it's a rich chocolate cake, hot chocolate, or chocolate fondue for plunging natural products, the guilty pleasure is important for the colder time of year experience.

- Groundhog-molded Treats

Groundhog-molded adds an eccentric touch to any festival, particularly for Groundhog Day. Here are a few inventive thoughts for creating these magnificent treats:

1. Groundhog Cookies:

Heat sugar treats looking like groundhogs utilizing a groundhog-molded cutout. Design with icing to add subtleties like eyes, fur, and the notable buckteeth.

2. Groundhog Cupcakes:

   Prepare cupcakes and embellish them with groundhog-themed clinchers. You can utilize fondant or chocolate to make adorable groundhog faces with ears jumping out.

3. Groundhog Cake Pops:

   Form cake jumps into groundhog shapes involving a round base for the body and little projections for the ears. Dunk them in chocolate or candy melts and add facial highlights utilizing consumable markers or little confections.

4. Groundhog Brownies:

   Cut brownies into groundhog shapes utilizing a stencil or freehand. Add chocolate icing for fur and facial elements. On the other hand, use fondant for a smoother finish.

5. Groundhog Pretzel Rods:

Dunk pretzel bars in chocolate, leaving a part undipped to act as the groundhog's body. Add subtleties involving different hued chocolates or icing for the face, ears, and tail.

6. Groundhog Rice Krispie Treats:

Shape Rice Krispie treats into groundhog structures, either freehand or utilizing a form. Enhance with chocolate and icing to draw out the highlights.

7. Groundhog Donuts:

Utilize a round doughnut as the base for the groundhog's face. Add edible eyes, a chocolate nose, and a line of icing to make the fur and mouth.

8. Groundhog Organic product Skewers:
Make sound groundhog-themed treats by piercing natural products like grapes, strawberries, and melon balls. Add eyes and a nose to the top grape to look like a groundhog's face.

9. Groundhog-molded Sandwiches:
   Make groundhog-molded sandwiches utilizing a groundhog-formed cutout. Fill them with the most loved fixings and utilize little consumable things like olives or cherry tomatoes for eyes and nose.

10. Groundhog Marshmallow Pops:
   Stick marshmallows onto sticks, dunk them in chocolate, and utilize palatable markers or icing to make groundhog faces. These make for a charming and delicious treat.

These groundhog-molded treats are delectable as well as add a bubbly and fun-loving component to your Groundhog Day festivities or any colder time of year-themed assembling.

CHAPTER 6: GROUNDHOG DAY REALITIES AND FANTASIES

- Exposing Normal Convictions

1. Vitamin C Fixes the Normal Cold:

While L-ascorbic acid is fundamental for a solid-resistant framework, taking exorbitant sums doesn't guarantee to fix or forestall the normal virus. It might diminish the term or seriousness of side effects at times, yet it's anything but an idiot-proof cure.

2. Humans Just Utilize 10% of Their Brains:

This far-reaching legend proposes that we have undiscovered mental potential. Truly, useful cerebrum imaging shows that different pieces of the mind have explicit capabilities, and there is no proof to help the idea of a 90% unused limit.

3. Shaving Causes Hair to Develop Thicker:

Shaving doesn't modify the thickness or pace of hair development. The impression of thicker hair is because of the unpolished edge of recently shaved hair, giving it a coarser vibe. Hair is not set in stone by hereditary qualities and chemicals.

4. Cracking Knuckles Causes Arthritis:

As opposed to mainstream thinking, there is no proof connecting knuckle breaking to joint pain. The sound is brought about by the arrival of gas rises in the synovial liquid inside joints and doesn't hurt the actual joint.

5. You Can Work Out Toxins:

Perspiring is a characteristic substantial cycle that manages internal heat levels. While it ousts some waste, working out poisons, particularly through unambiguous detox techniques, is generally confusing. The liver and kidneys assume more critical parts in detoxification.

6. Eating Carrots Further develops Night Vision:
Carrots are plentiful in vitamin A, which is fundamental for eye well-being, yet consuming unnecessary sums will not mystically upgrade night vision. This conviction comes from The Second Great War promulgation elevating carrot utilization to mask the utilization of radar innovation.

7. Reading in Faint Light Demolishes Eyesight:
Perusing in faint light might cause eye strain and exhaustion, however, it doesn't prompt

extremely durable harm or the requirement for glasses. Changing lighting conditions or utilizing legitimate bifocals can reduce eye distress.

8. Hair and Nails Keep on Becoming After Death:

The thought that hair and nails develop after death is a fantasy. The presence of development is because of a lack of hydration and the withdrawal of skin, causing hair and nails to appear to be longer.

9. Sugar Causes Hyperactivity in Children:

Various examinations have exposed the possibility that sugar straightforwardly causes hyperactivity in youngsters. A self-influenced consequence and situational factors are more probable supporters of the view of the expanded movement in the wake of devouring sweet food sources.

10. Goldfish Have a Three-Second Memory:

Goldfish have a more extended memory range than three seconds. Research recommends they can recollect things for quite a long time and even months, scattering the legend that their memory is very brief.

- Uncommon Groundhog Day Stories

1. Jimmy the Groundhog's City chairman Mishap:

In 2015, the city chairman of Sun Grassland, Wisconsin, was chomped by Jimmy the Groundhog during the Groundhog Day function. The city chairman, Jonathan Freund, was holding Jimmy when the groundhog clamped down on his ear. Regardless of the startling episode, the city hall leader went on with the merriments, and both he and Jimmy were fine.

2. Chattanooga Toss' Late-winter Prediction:
   Chattanooga Toss, a groundhog from Tennessee, stood out as truly newsworthy in 2016 by foreseeing a late winter. This takeoff from the conventional six additional long stretches of winter earned consideration and added a curve to the standard Groundhog Day conjectures.

3. Balzac Billy's Canadian Winter Forecast:
   In Balzac, Alberta, Canada, Balzac Billy is the neighborhood climate foreseeing groundhog. In 2018, he anticipated a late winter yet in addition anticipated six additional long stretches of

political unrest, infusing a comical and effective component into the custom.

4. Staten Island Throw's Disputable Drop:

In 2014, Staten Island Throw, the groundhog from New York, slipped from the city hall leader's hands during the Groundhog Day function and tumbled to the ground. Luckily, Throw was safe, however the occurrence ignited a touch of debate and humor in the media.

5. French Stream Freddie's Blizzard Forecast:

In West Virginia, French Stream Freddie is known for his climate expectations. In 2015, he estimated six additional long stretches of winter and the exceptionally following day, the district encountered a huge blizzard. Freddie's precise expectation added a dash of persona to the Groundhog Day legend.

6. Pothole Phil's Non-Climate Predictions:

Pothole Phil, a groundhog from Michigan, became popular not so much for climate expectations but rather for foreseeing the number of potholes the district would have. This idiosyncratic methodology added a silly contort to the conventional Groundhog Day merriments.

7. Dunkirk Dave's Association in Lawful Dispute:

Dunkirk Dave, a groundhog from New York, became entangled in a lawful question in 2019. The conflict included two contending groundhog overseers, each professing to be the authority guardian of Dunkirk Dave. The fight in court focused on the regularly happy practice.

CHAPTER 7: NATURAL VIEWPOINTS

- Groundhogs and Environments

Groundhogs, otherwise called woodchucks, assume huge parts in environments, adding to biodiversity and impacting vegetation elements. Here are a few manners by which groundhogs cooperate with their biological systems:

1. Burrow Creation:

Groundhogs are talented burrowers, making broad passage frameworks that act as their homes. These tunnels, with different doors and loads, give cover not exclusively to groundhogs but additionally to other little creatures like bunnies, skunks, and foxes.

2. Vegetation Impact:

Groundhogs are herbivores and fundamentally affect vegetation. They consume different plants, including grasses, clover, and horticultural harvests. Their taking care of propensities can impact plant creation and thickness in the areas they possess.

3. Seed Dispersal:

Groundhogs inadvertently add to seed dispersal as they travel through various living spaces. Seeds can append to their fur or be kept through their excrement, supporting the spread of plant species across scenes.

4. Predator-Prey Relationships:

Groundhogs are important for the food web, filling in as prey for different hunters like foxes, coyotes, flying predators, and snakes. Their presence adds to the equilibrium of hunter-prey connections inside biological systems.

5. Soil Aeration:

The digging exercises of groundhogs assist with circulating air through the dirt, advancing better water invasion and root development for plants. This can decidedly affect soil design and by and large environment wellbeing.

6. Temperature Regulation:

Groundhog tunnels give a stable and protected climate, permitting them to control their internal heat level and break outrageous weather patterns. Different creatures may likewise involve these tunnels for temperature guidelines and security.

7. Behavioral Adaptations:

Groundhogs display social variations, like hibernation throughout the cold weather months. This conduct assists them with saving energy as well as impacts the accessibility of food assets for different creatures during the colder seasons.

8. Ecosystem Resilience:
Groundhogs, as biological system engineers, add to the flexibility of their living spaces. The adjustments they make to their current circumstance through tunnel development and scavenging exercises can affect the design and capability of biological systems.

- Preservation Endeavors

While groundhogs are not commonly viewed as jeopardized, protection endeavors frequently center around saving and keeping up with biodiversity inside biological systems, and this incorporates the prosperity of groundhogs. Here are some broad protection standards and contemplations:

1. Habitat Preservation:

Safeguarding normal territories is vital for groundhog populations. Protection endeavors expect to safeguard and reestablish regions with appropriate territories, guaranteeing there are adequate rooms for groundhogs to lay out tunnels and rummage.

2. Wildlife Corridors:

Making natural life passages or availability between living spaces assists groundhogs and different species with moving openly, lessening the effect of territory discontinuity. This is especially significant in urbanized or horticultural scenes.

3. Educational Programs:

Protection associations frequently execute instructive projects to bring issues to light about the significance of groundhogs and their part in environments. Instructing the public aides cultivates a more prominent comprehension of these creatures and supports dependable concurrence.

4. Research and Monitoring:

Progressing exploration and checking drives give important information on groundhog populaces, conduct, and well-being. This data is basic for going with informed protection choices and evaluating the effect of human exercises on groundhog natural surroundings.

5. Management of Human-Untamed Life Conflict:

As groundhogs can now and again be viewed as nuisances, successful and accommodating techniques for overseeing human-natural life struggles are fundamental. Protection endeavors might include executing procedures that limit negative connections without hurting the creatures.

6. Protection from Disease:

Checking and dealing with the spread of infections that can influence groundhog populations is essential. Moderates work to comprehend and relieve likely dangers from sicknesses that might influence groundhogs and other untamed life.

7. Invasive Species Control:

Controlling obtrusive species that might disturb groundhog living spaces or seek assets is important for protection endeavors. This keeps up with the equilibrium of environments and guarantees that local verdure flourish.

8. Climate Change Mitigation:

Tending to the effects of environmental change is fundamental for the drawn-out protection of groundhog territories. Preservationists work on drives that advance environment versatility and transformation for natural life populations.

9. Legislation and Strategy Advocacy:

Preservation associations frequently advocate for defensive regulation and arrangements that protect natural life territories and direct exercises that could antagonistically influence groundhog populaces.

10. Collaboration with Communities:

Drawing in with neighborhood networks is fundamental for fruitful protection endeavors. Joint effort assists work with supporting preservation drives, empowers capable land use, and cultivates a feeling of shared liability regarding safeguarding biodiversity.

CHAPTER 8: GROUNDHOG DAY IN 2024

- Features of the Day's Occasions

Here are the features of the day's occasions:

1. Groundhog Development Ceremony:

The day started with the eagerly awaited Groundhog Day function. Participants accumulated at the assigned area to observe the groundhog rising out of its tunnel, enthusiastically anticipating the climate expectation.

2. Phil's Prediction:

The superstar, Punxsutawney Phil, showed up. Everyone's attention was on Phil as he either saw his shadow or not, giving the yearly weather conditions conjecture. The declaration produced energy and expectation among the group.

3. Festive Atmosphere:

The occasion was set apart by a happy air, with unrecorded music, diversion, and different exercises for participants. Neighborhood merchants and food slow down added to the celebratory soul, offering a scope of treats and trinkets.

4. Inner Circle Ceremony:

The Inward Circle, a gathering of neighborhood dignitaries liable for Phil's consideration, assumed a vital part in the day's occasions. They coordinated the service, deciphered Phil's forecast, and drew in with the group to upgrade the general insight.

5. Community Involvement:

Groundhog Day isn't just about climate expectations; it's a local area festivity. Nearby occupants, guests, and families met up to partake in the merriments, creating a feeling of fellowship and custom.

6. Media Coverage:

The occasion got broad media inclusion, with journalists catching the fervor, interviews with coordinators, and responses from the group. The practice's worldwide allure was obvious through the inclusion of different media sources.

7. Cultural References:

Groundhog Day frequently incorporates gestures to the film "Groundhog Day." Whether it's referenced in addresses, outfits, or occasion embellishments, the social effect of the film is woven into the texture of the festival.

8. Groundhog-Themed Treats:

Neighborhood organizations and sellers offered groundhog-molded treats, adding a lively and imaginative component to the culinary contributions. Groundhog-molded treats, cupcakes, and different joys were delighted in by participants.

9. Weather Aficionados and Tourists:

The occasion pulled in climate aficionados and vacationers from all over. Individuals headed out to encounter the special practice, adding to the different and exuberant group.

10. Positive People group Spirit:

One of the day's features was the positive local area soul. Whether it was the cheers following Phil's forecast or the common chuckling during merriments, Groundhog Day united individuals in a festival of custom and climate legends.

- Public Responses and Online Entertainment Buzz

Public responses and online entertainment buzz encompassing Groundhog Day were lively and different, mirroring the occasion's inescapable allure. Here is a brief look into the excited reactions:

1. Anticipation and Excitement:
Individuals communicated elevated degrees of expectation and energy paving the way to

Punxsutawney Phil's climate forecast. Virtual entertainment stages were swirling with commencements, GIFs, and images catching the excitement of the crowd.

2. Live Streaming and Updates:

Numerous people couldn't go to the occasion in that frame of mind on live streaming and constant reports via virtual entertainment stages. This permitted a worldwide crowd to partake in the experience.

3. Humorous Images and Jokes:

Web-based entertainment clients overflowed stages with hilarious images and jokes connected with Groundhog Day. Images highlighting Punxsutawney Phil references to the film "Groundhog Day," and perky pokes at the unconventionality of climate expectations became viral.

4. Weather Lovers' Insights:

Climate lovers and meteorologists took part in conversations about the meaning of Phil's expectations. A few common bits of knowledge into the meteorological perspectives, examining weather conditions and the legends encompassing Groundhog Day.

5. Community Engagement:

Neighborhood people groups and associations effectively partook in the web-based discussions. They shared in the background glimpses, and occasion features, and urged devotees to participate in the festival utilizing committed hashtags.

6. Creative Hashtags:

Web-based entertainment clients made and embraced innovative hashtags connected with Groundhog Day, working with a firm internet-based discussion. Hashtags like #GroundhogDay, #PhilPredicts, and #WeatherWhiskers moved as individuals shared their contemplations and encounters.

7. Groundhog-Themed Challenges:
Online difficulties and challenges with a groundhog topic got some decent forward momentum. Members shared photographs of groundhog-formed treats, Do-It-Yourself groundhog embellishments, and innovative translations of Punxsutawney Phil.

8. Cultural References to the Movie:

References to the film "Groundhog Day" were common in web-based conversations. Clients cited notorious lines, shared GIFs from the film, and, surprisingly, reproduced scenes, adding a nostalgic and mainstream society aspect to the web-based entertainment buzz.

9. Positive People group Spirit:

The general tone via web-based entertainment mirrored a positive local area soul. Individuals commended the extraordinary practice, shared their own Groundhog Day customs, and associated with other people who valued the eccentricity of the occasion.

10. Global Participation:

Groundhog Day's worldwide allure was obvious in online entertainment connections. Clients from various nations shared their viewpoints, in some cases drawing matches with their nearby practices or communicating interest in the exceptionally American festival.

CONCLUSION

Groundhog Day is something beyond an eccentric custom; a social peculiarity unites networks, sparkles fervor, and adds a dash of caprice to the colder time of year. The day's occasions, from the enthusiastically anticipated development service to Punxsutawney Phil's climate forecast, make an exceptional mix of fables, meteorology, and local area festivity.

The public responses and online entertainment buzz further enhance the occasion's effect, displaying a worldwide crowd enthusiastically captivating in conversations, sharing humor, and taking part in aggregate expectations. Groundhog Day has turned into a common encounter that rises above geological limits, with individuals from different foundations meeting up to commend custom and climate old stories.

The positive local area soul, clear in the celebrations, mirrors an aggregate appreciation for the cheerful and shared parts of Groundhog Day. The day's features, including groundhog-themed treats, social references, and a different scope of exercises, add to the persevering appeal of this yearly festival.

While Punxsutawney Phil's climate forecast stays a fun-loving and informal part of the practice, Groundhog Day fills in as a sign of the significance of the local shared customs, and the delight gained from embracing the unforeseen. Whether going to the function face to face or taking part basically through online entertainment, people from varying backgrounds

Groundhog Day

meet up to delight in the imp

impossible-to-missed wonderful soul of

Groundhog Day.